Hereward College

LEARNING RESOURCES
CENTRE

For Anita

THE
OUTLANDISH ADVENTURES
∞ OF ORPHEUS IN ∞
THE UNDERWORLD

by
PAUL NEWHAM

Illustrations by
ELAINE COX

BAREFOOT BOOKS
BOSTON & BATH

FOREWORD

—∞—

The character of Orpheus originates in Greek mythology. The Greeks adored and worshipped Orpheus as the father of song and as such the carrier of a special kind of healing. In Greek culture, music was believed to possess medicinal powers, and the close connection between music and health is represented mythically by Orpheus's brother Asclepius being the father of medicine.

The curative power of song has been recognized and embraced by many cultures where singing forms a significant part of healing rituals. Although our Western culture has divorced music from medicine, most people are greatly moved when they listen to a singing voice, an experience that puts them in touch with their deepest feelings. According to the many writers who recorded Orpheus's adventures, his songs proved capable of freezing enemies, calming aggressors, putting raging creatures to sleep, taming animals, and charming women. In the popular story of Jason and the Argonauts, the hypnotic voice of Orpheus is able to bring the approaching enemies to a standstill when clubs, swords, and arrows fail. Yet Orpheus cannot be compared with the aggressive male heroes of Greek myth, such as Jason, Hercules, or Achilles. He is essentially a pacifist; and his strength lies not in the use of violence or military tactics, but in his ability to calm and arrest the violent instinct in others.

The most popular adventure of Orpheus, which has been the subject of some of the greatest paintings, poetry, and music for over two thousand years, is that which tells of his love for Eurydice. It is through his singing that Orpheus captures the heart of Eurydice and it is through music that they are joined in love. Then Eurydice is bitten by a serpent and taken in death to the underworld, where no person alive may enter and from which no one dead can return. But Orpheus dares to follow her into the underworld, where he encounters a number of daunting obstacles. He must persuade Charon the ferryman to take him across the raging river Styx; pass Cerberus, the three-headed hound; and, of course, win the stony heart of Hades, god of the underworld, so as to secure his lover's release.

It is not only in the story of Orpheus, but in myths worldwide that we find such a mysterious underworld peopled by creatures with special powers and foreboding characteristics, and against whom the hero must pit his strength. However, what makes Orpheus's journey particularly inspiring and unusual is that it is entirely through the transformative power of song that he is able to confront and overcome the threats which he discovers there. So compelling are his songs that they persuade Charon to steer him across the Styx. So sweet is his voice that it entices Cerberus to direct him to the heart of the underworld. So placating is his music that it moves Hades to allow light to enter where darkness has always prevailed, and to permit Orpheus to take Eurydice back to the light of day.

A condition of Orpheus being allowed to do this is that he does not turn to look at Eurydice until they are once more under the sun of the upper world. However, while undergoing the difficult journey from the underworld to the upper world and unable to resist looking back, he turns to assure himself of her safety and so loses her forever. When Orpheus returns to the light of day without his beloved, he learns to express his mourning in the form of music and song, and through this is able to evoke the presence of Eurydice inside himself, a presence which can never be taken away from him.

Therefore it is not only through song that Orpheus discovers his love and is able to rescue her when she is first lost to him, but, more poignantly, it is also through the healing capacity of song that he recovers from his bereavement at the second and final loss of his dearest Eurydice.

The transformative power of song in the myth of Orpheus is a power which is also present in our everyday lives, if we know how to take advantage of it. Singing has always been a means of giving voice to powerful emotion. We can sing as an expression of our most positive and uplifting experiences as well as a way of releasing deep sadness. Through song we can awaken the memory of lovers and friends, enhance special times of intimacy, and recover from the effects of catastrophe and loss. To hear an expressive voice or to use song, in whatever way, to express ourselves has a purging influence upon our soul. The song is a great healer.

That Orpheus should find recovery in song not only reflects a belief in the curative power of music, but also exemplifies a vital fact of life, as relevant today as always. We all must and will experience loss; through loss we mourn, through mourning we express our sadness, and through our sadness we grow toward recovery and self-fulfillment. The story of Orpheus has something fundamental to give to us. It testifies to the value of song as a means of gaining love, strength, and self-development, and by implication reminds us of the indispensable vitality of all art.

Paul Newham

THE OUTLANDISH ADVENTURES OF
∞ ORPHEUS IN THE UNDERWORLD ∞

Forever and today in the far far west,
rugged lands and wooded valleys
roll out under a raging sun.
Fathomless sea lashes silvery sands
and salt-white sails steer gold-cargoed ships.
The days are long with work and the nights
are rich with love song.
Here in this glorious time, and this golden land,
the god Apollo and the fair Calliope
gave birth to a baby boy
and his name was Orpheus.

As Orpheus grew to manhood
his skin remained smooth as newly washed pebbles;
his hair cascaded in sunny locks and curls;
his lush green eyes looked deep into all that they saw
and he marveled at the world.
Orpheus was gentle and generous;
he was never tricked or tempted
into scraps or scrapes, battles or brawls;
he always found a clever way out of a difficult corner.

Orpheus was loved
by the animals of desert and forest;
by the birds in the looming blue skies;
and by the creatures who brood in boggledy, burrowed tunnels
beneath the rain-sodden earth.
These creatures feared the men who come
with clumpy cluggedy feet and cudgels
to slug down the helpless four-legged roamers
and two-winged flyers.

Orpheus did not wish to kill and eat wild creatures
but to roam with them and learn their language
of squeaks and roars, calls and cries, barks and whispers.
Day and night he wandered the wild hills
quietly watching, quietly awake.
So trusted and close to the animals was Orpheus
that the white-winged chelladoor settled on his shoulder
and the claw-footed gudthubber ate from his open hand.

Orpheus was the priceless jewel of his parents' heart.
When his son grew to manhood
Apollo offered him a special gift,
as all fathers offer their sons.
Apollo thought of shields and swords and fighting horses and racing shoes
and even a golden chariot.
But Orpheus was above war and treachery;
he did not wish to race or drive with whip and wheel.
Orpheus preferred to talk to the animals and celebrate the wild world.

So Apollo gave him a wonderful lyre.
Its strings were plucked from the tail of a fine white stallion
and its body was carved from rich dark oak;
and the moment Orpheus strummed the lyre
a voluptuous music rang out
so that all who heard it were rapt with joy and sorrow.
Orpheus opened his throat and sighed with pleasure,
and the most beautiful honey-gold song
resounded in glides and curves
serenading every woman, man, child, and creature.

Now came the time for Orpheus
to thank his father and embrace his mother
and depart his homeland in search of love.
With pack and lyre in hand
sure-footed Orpheus set out for the deep south.
As he made his way through woodland and plain
Orpheus discovered that his songs
were imbued with special powers.
When the hot sun baked the soft moss underfoot too hard,
Orpheus's cavernous tones raised a storm of quenching rain.
When the storm raged too fiercely,
the whispering waves of Orpheus's voice
calmed the howling winds and turned pelting torrents to soft showers.
When thieves, rogues, or wayward men approached him,
Orpheus's song would lull them to sleep
and he would tiptoe on while they dozed.
Orpheus found in his voice and his song
a greater power than all the shields and swords and horses
and fast-footed racing shoes and golden chariots
that other men prize;
for with his voice he could protect himself
without causing harm.

When Orpheus had traveled for a hundred and one days,
his ears caught the sound of an unfamiliar tune.
Orpheus was astonished – and enraptured.
He leaned against the bark of a towering cedar
and peered around to where the sweet sound arose.
Orpheus was immediately mesmerized
by the astounding beauty he saw there.
A woman in golden-brown and crimson cloth
glided and turned in grace and splendor,
singing a song which told of her longing
to discover a man whom she could love
and hold close to her heart.
As she danced her hair swirled and twirled,
her swan-like neck rippled and curved
and her arms swooped and waved
and her legs spun and spun.
Orpheus watched –
and Orpheus sighed.

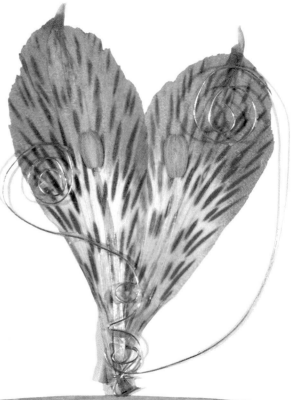

At once the dancer stopped.
She and Orpheus stood before one another.
They did not touch; they did not move.
They stared into each other's eyes
as endless tunnels leading deeper and deeper
into their bottomless hearts.
Slowly, sweetly
they touched and kissed and danced,
not like two people, but like one.
His songs beckoned her to be ever nearer to him,
and within the waxing of the next full moon
they were married beneath the splendid heavens
and the night sky blessed them with true happiness
born from true love.

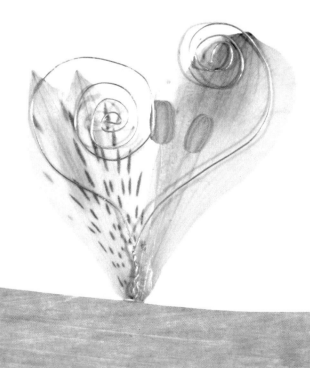

But the love-filled days which Orpheus shared with Eurydice
were soon to be stolen.
In the late dusk of a mid-spring evening
Orpheus lay slumbering beneath a lemon tree
and Eurydice roamed into the forest's heartland
to gather berries and nuts.
The evening grew long
and with the night came a thick and smoldering fog.
Eurydice could barely see the outline of the nearest bush.
She felt the grip of an ugly hand upon her shoulder
and she smelled the foul breath of a creature
whose whiskers brushed against her cheek
as its hands slid around her.
Eurydice smattered and smote with arms and legs
and breaking free she ran and ran, now this way, now that.
She struck the sturdy trunk of a sniddling tree
and crashed to the forest floor.
In the hollow of this sniddling tree
a snidy serpent lived.

With his sniggling snattering eyes
the serpent saw the fair sweet skin of woman
and he slithered down and pierced her elbow
with his poison.
Now Eurydice could not awaken again.
Like all who die in the far far west
she was transported by the dark dark winds
through the great gorging crag
down the echoing blackness
through the earth's floor
across the river Styx
and into the underworld –
a weird and wild place ruled by the invisible one
whose name is Hades.

Orpheus awoke to find his beloved gone.

He sought her in the forest

first by the washing pool and then in the vale of berries,

then on the twinding path east, then on the straight path west.

When he came upon the sturdy trunk of the sniddling tree where the snidy serpent lived,

he knew at once that Eurydice had died.

Now, he knew, she was in the underworld –

a place where all who die must go, never to return;

a place where no one who lives can ever venture.

Orpheus' heavy heart heaved and thumped and beat

with despair and regret and rage.

His throat was clogged and clammy and sadness ensnared him.

He could not eat, he could not drink.

His breath grew cold and turned his voice to mournful sighs.

Then he remembered he could sing.

If, with his voice,

he could stop the floods and calm the furious storms,

perhaps he could sing his way to the underworld,

rescue Eurydice, and return her to earth?

Orpheus traced his lover's footsteps

through the great gorging crag

down the echoing blackness

through the earth's floor

and into the underworld.

After an age of falling

he landed at the shore of the river Styx.

The river Styx is a putrid swamp

which bubbles and belches and spurts thick black spittle.

The only way across is in the only boat in all the underworld owned, guarded, and

crewed by Charon the ferryman.

Charon's bones are as brittle as charcoal.
His skin is crumpled and corrugated,
his eyes are as the color of pig's skin
and his voice is like the cracking and spitting
of burning wood.
"I will not let you cross," snarkeled Charon,
"for you are not dead
and the land of Hades is no place for the living."

Orpheus drew his lyre from its pack.
He sang a song about brave old boatmen
who dare to sail through difficult waters.
Charon was entranced.
He remembered the sailing he had done
in his younger years
and he beckoned Orpheus aboard.
Though the vessel rocked and veered
against the grimy waves of grunge,
Orpheus sang on
until they reached the other side.

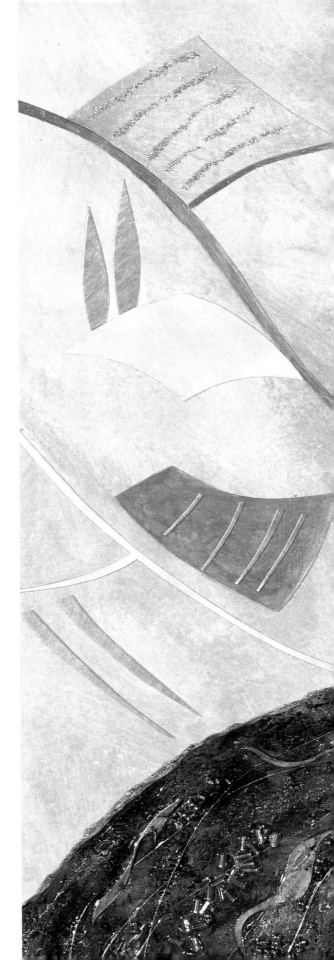

As the oars came to rest
Charon realized that he had delivered a living man to the place of the dead
and feared for Orpheus' safety.
"Beware," he said,
"for though you are now safely across the river Styx,
you must now get past the three-headed hound of Hades.
His name is Cerberus
and he may not be so moved by your melody as I."
The great teeth of Cerberus crunched and clankered –
canine gnashing gnawlers that snarled and smattered
like mammoth castle gates hung on hinges of gristle and bone.
His three mammoth snozils had nostrils like volcanoes
and he sniffed out Orpheus long before our grand hero could see him.

His hooked galloping legs pounced and pranced in a dance of delirious delight
at the prospect of the sumptuous meal that was approaching.
His needles of steely hair bristled and bunched
and his ears flapped like pirate sails
in the cold and merciless wind of the underworld.
Orpheus did not tremble.
Each time Cerberus barked or whimpered
Orpheus played a note on his lyre and shared the canine song.
So much did the three-headed hound enjoy this song and dance
that his three lengthy tongues licked Orpheus' cheek
and he led Orpheus by a short cut
to the center of the underworld.

Orpheus found himself on a rocky jutted platform
suspended between two chalk staircases.
From this platform he could see the two sides of the underworld.
Down the staircase to his left was the bright place
where waterfalls cascade and fruit trees blossom.
Down the staircase to his right was darkness.
Orpheus stared into the blackness.
He saw Sisyphus
rolling with bare and bleeding hands
a thundering global stone,
heavy as a mountain, high as a cliff,
to the top of a mighty hill.
But each and every time,
the rock would instantly carundle down the hill
dragging Sisyphus grudduggering down,
to begin all over again.

He saw the three Danaids
as they filled a giant jug full to the brim with water.
But as fast as the women poured,
the water sprayed its escape
through a thousand and one holes.

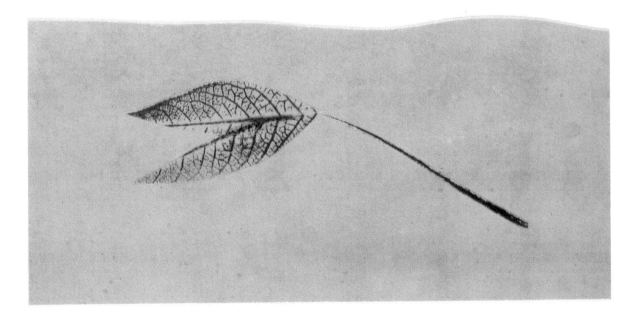

He saw Tantalus
stranded on a rock beneath a glistening citrus tree
at the shore of a fresh-water lake,
parched with thirst and ravenous with hunger,
forever tantalized and tempted
to reach upward for the fruit and downward for the water.
Whenever his spindled and fleshless fingers
came close to grasping the twangy lemonine buds,
a cunning wind would sweep the branch beyond his reach;
and whenever he stooped downward toward the lake,
the tide of the moon would draw the water away
leaving bare and barren sand.

Orpheus was staggered and stuck in his boots
at the sight of these terrible trials
and he sung a song of sympathy from the depths of his heart.

Far away in the canyons of light
Eurydice recognized her dear lover's voice
and cried out to be with him once more.
Now for the first time in all eternity
Hades was moved to soften his stern and stubborn stance.
For the song of Orpheus touched his ears as no song had before.
So softened was the hard and hostile heart of Hades
that he allowed Sisyphus and all who toiled to stop their tasks
and brought a shaft of radiant light
to shine on the dark side of the underworld.

Orpheus saw his chance.
Making the most of Hades' rare generosity,
he begged him to allow Eurydice
to follow him back to the upper world
and to the light of day.
"You know that no one returns upward
once they have fallen into the clutches of Hades,"
the screeching voice whistled,
"but I will make an exception this time
and on one condition.
I will allow Eurydice to follow behind you
on your journey back across the river Styx,
up through the echoing blackness,
through the great gorging crag to the upper world.
But you must not at any time turn around to look at your beloved
until you are under the full day's sun –
else she is mine forever."

Orpheus turned
and walked steadily back the way he had come.
He was forever tempted to turn
and adore his long-lost soul mate
but he forced himself to find content
in the sound of her footsteps behind him
and the warmth of her breath on the back of his neck.
Up passage and down crater,
through pot holes and clagons they walked in single file
until they met Charon at the shore of the river Styx.
The ferryman steered them across the black waters
as they sat back to back,
not daring to look into each other's eyes.
The ferryman left them and wished them luck.

Then came the final
and most fatal
part of their journey.
As no one ever left the underworld,
the steep echoing blackness
that led to the earth's floor
was a sheer and slippery climb
for anyone going upward;
with no grips or footholds
or protruding twaglets to grasp.
Orpheus splayed arms and legs outward
pressing them into the vertical walls.
He heaved himself upward hoping,
moment by moment,
that Eurydice would do the same.

Orpheus climbed with all his might
 and longed with all his heart
for Eurydice to follow him.
As he heaved and climbed
he longed to hold and help her.

He looked back
to see if she was safe . . .
At that moment the implacable winds of Hades
snatched Eurydice a second and final time,
never to be seen or touched or smelled by Orpheus again.
Alone once more in the upper world,
Orpheus sobbed and cried and shed many tears
for his lost beloved.
His sobs led to notes and his notes led to love songs,
and when Orpheus sang he felt Eurydice awaken deep within his heart
as though she were still with him.
His songs echoed in the trees and through the valleys
and in the echoes he heard Eurydice reply.
Once again his beautiful honey-gold music
resounded in glides and curves
serenading every woman, man, child, and creature.

Forever and today in the far far west
some say that in the long valley of citrus trees
you can still hear the echoes of his songs in the wind.

BAREFOOT BOOKS

the children's books imprint of

Shambhala Publications, Inc.

Horticultural Hall

300 Massachusetts Avenue

Boston, Massachusetts 02115

This book has been printed on 100% acid-free paper

Printed in Belgium by Proost International Book Production

Text © 1993 by Paul Newham

Illustrations © 1993 by Elaine Cox

First published in Great Britain in 1993 by Barefoot Books Ltd

First published in the United States of America in 1994 by Shambhala Publications, Inc.

ISBN 1–56957–908–3

9 8 7 6 5 4 3 2 1

Distributed in the United States by Random House, Inc.,

and in Canada by Random House of Canada Ltd